MY FIRST

COLUMBUS DAY BOOK

by Dee Lillegard
illustrated by Betty Raskin

created by The Child's World

CHILDRENS PRESS ®
CHICAGO

Library of Congress Cataloging in Publication Data

Lillegard, Dee.
    My first Columbus Day book.

    Summary: Recounts in verse how Christopher Columbus
planned and executed his voyage west, resulting in the
claiming of new lands for Spain.
        1. Columbus, Christopher—Juvenile literature.
    2. Explorers—America—Biography—Juvenile literature.
    3. Explorers—Spain—Biography—Juvenile literature.
    4. America—Discovery and exploration—Spanish—Juvenile
literature.   [1. Columbus, Christopher.   2. Explorers.
3. America—Discovery and exploration—Spanish]
I. Raskin, Betty, ill.   II. Child's World (Firm)
III. Title.
E111.L767   1987   970.01'5 [92]   87-10304
ISBN 0-516-02909-6

MY FIRST

COLUMBUS DAY BOOK

A Childhood Dream

In Genoa, in Italy, Christopher
    first saw the sea.
In Genoa, in Italy, Christopher
    knew what he wanted to be.
Not a weaver, like his father and
    mother—
He had a whole new world to
    discover.
In Genoa, in Italy, Christopher
    knew what he *had* to be—
    an explorer!

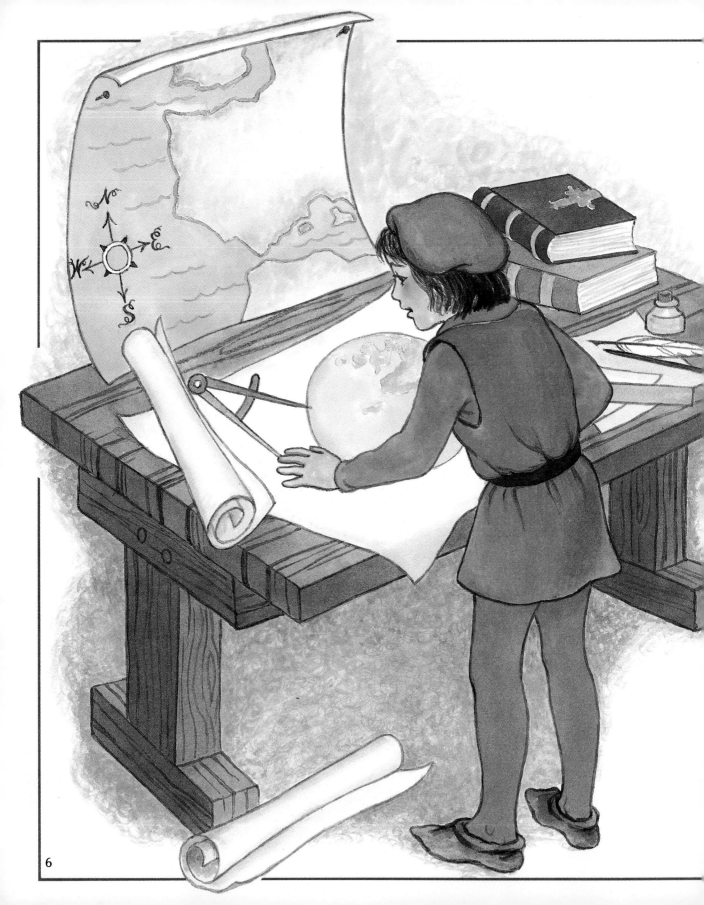

Round or Flat?

Some people thought the world
     was flat,
But Christopher Columbus knew
     better than that.
"Listen! Listen!" Christopher said.
"Get that idea out of your head.
I've studied maps and charts
     and found
That the earth, like a great big ball,
     is *round*!"

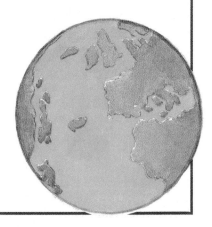

A New Way

"We need spices from the Indies,"
The people of Europe said.
"But a war-like nation stops us
From traveling east by land."

"There's another way," said Columbus,
"To get to the Indies from here.
Sail west. And since the earth is round,
    not flat or square,
You'll soon have all the spices you lack.
I'll show you—I'll *sail* to the Indies
    and *back*!"

Kings and Queens

Columbus needed money
To sail to the Indies and so. . .
He asked the king of Portugal.
But the king's answer was, "No.

The French also told him, "No."
So Columbus took his maps
To Ferdinand and Isabella of Spain.
Their answer was, "Perhaps. . . ."

"Our country is at war," they said.
"Our troubles are too great.
Perhaps when the war is over. . .
Wait, Columbus, wait."

Don't Give Up

"Don't give up!"
Said Columbus' son.
He believed in his father . . .
In what could be done.

One year passed,
Two years, and more.
Columbus waited patiently
While Spain fought the war.

Columbus waited—*seven years*.
Then, at last—success!
Spain won the war, and her
    king and queen
Said, "Yes, Columbus, yes!"

Finding Sailors

"Who will sail with Columbus?
Who will come along?"

"What if the world is really flat?
What if he is wrong?"

"Who will sail with Columbus?"

"I, sir!"

"And me, too!"

It wasn't easy—but he did it.
Columbus found his crew!

Three Ships

The Niña, the Pinta,
And grandest of all—
The Santa Maria,
With her sails so tall.

The Santa Maria,
Christopher's own,
In which to sail
So far from home.

Three ships for Columbus,
Brave and bold.
Three ships to the Indies
For spices. . .and gold!

Finally Ready

They loaded their ships
With rice and beans,
Fresh water and cheese,
Anchovies, sardines.

They were finally ready,
Columbus and his crew.
They sailed August third,
1492.

On the Water

Water and sky. Water and sky.
The sailors began to wonder why. . . .
Why were they sailing so far, so long?
"Let's go home, Columbus!
You're wrong! You're wrong!"

But Columbus stood firm.
He knew what was best.
"Sail on," he commanded.
"Sail on to the west."

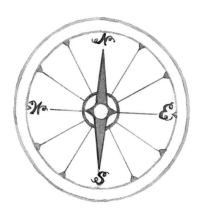

A New World

"Land!" someone shouted
In the early morning air.
Columbus, in the moonlight,
Saw that land was really there!

He led his sailors to the shore.
He knelt and kissed the ground.
He said a prayer of thanks to God
That they were safe and sound.

He thought he was in the Indies.
And so did all his crew
That Friday morning, October 12th,
1492!

October 1492

			1	2	3
4	5	6	7	8	9	10
11	12	13	14	15	16	17
18	19	20	21	22	23	24
25	26	27	28	29	30	31

Friendly Natives

Columbus thought he was in India.
But some things, to him, seemed odd.
He called the natives, "Indians."
They thought he was a god.

He gave them bright red caps to wear,
And shiny beads, and bells.
They gave him colorful parrots,
And bits of gold, and shells.

Their language was too different
For Columbus to understand.
But the natives were so friendly,
He felt welcome in their land.

A Royal Welcome

Home again! A big parade!
Columbus' treasures all displayed!

Parrots in cages. Trinkets of gold.
Baskets filled with all they could hold.

Flowers and plants and something sweet—
Pineapple! A brand new fruit to eat.

Columbus, on horseback, led the way,
Followed by Indian friends that day.

The king and queen declared that he
Was admiral of the ocean sea!

This prophecy was fulfilled by my father, the admiral, in the year 1492.

A Great New Land

"A great new continent will be found,"
Someone in Europe wrote. . .
Long before Columbus sailed.
Later, his son made a note:
    "This prophecy was fulfilled,"
He wrote, (proud that it was true),
"By my father. . .the admiral
    in. . .1492."

The Indies

He never reached the Indies.
He found new land instead.
But because of Columbus,
Other explorers said:

"Let's try to get to the Indies—
To India, China, Japan,
To the fabulous Spice Islands—
Let's follow Columbus' plan."

They wouldn't walk or ride;
        they'd sail.
The idea sounded good.
One day they finally did it
As Columbus said they could!